50 New & Traditional Wedding Vow Examples

Plus

How To Write Your Own Vows: 10 Guides

Marie Kay

TO MY PARENTS

Happily married for more than 50 years. You make it easy
to see the beauty of marriage vows, well-lived.

CONTENTS

"Don't walk in front of me, I may not follow.
Don't walk behind me, I may not lead.
Just walk beside me and be my friend."
- Albert Camus

"Doubt thou the stars are fire;
Doubt that the sun doth move;
Doubt truth to be a liar;
But never doubt I love."
- William Shakespeare, Hamlet

FORWARD

Some years ago, my brother and his bride used original vows in their wedding.

Not only did the couple write their own, they chose not to share them prior to the ceremony. When his bride got through speaking her vows of how wonderful she thought my brother was, my brother could not help himself but to say – out loud, "Wow. Thanks!"

She brought him to attention, and he...brought the house down. It wouldn't have been so funny if it hadn't been such an honest a response from him. So yes, everyone listens to your vows, especially your betrothed.

Now for the tricky part. According to a Gallup survey, 40% of Americans fear speaking in public in front of an audience.[i] So, it's no wonder that proclaiming one's wedding vows to a captive congregation can be a stressor.

Compound this by an earnest desire to compose them personally, and you may have a great case of writer's block.

The good news is, take a systematic approach, and you'll be a poet in no time.

With a little love, a few memories, and maybe some inspiration from those who've gone before, you may compose vows so lovely they're well remembered, or even emulated. Your mate might even say, "Wow, thanks."

Congratulations, and enjoy.

1
WHAT IS A VOW?

A little background…

According to Webster's Dictionary, a *vow* is a solemn promise or assertion; specifically: one by which a person is bound to an act, service or condition.

Its first known use was in the 13th century, from Middle English. This means that prior to that, vows weren't even necessarily a part of the marriage institution.

As far back as the first century couples were "betrothed" for perhaps a year, getting to know one another, culminating in a sexual consummation of the marriage, and a big party about it.

So much for assuming "it's always been vows and white dresses."

Why the heck is this important? Because it

means that the definition of "vow" is not necessarily something that has always been prescribed.

A vow, truly and simply means, *whatever promise binds you.*

THE CLASSIC, TRADITIONAL WEDDING VOWS, AND WHERE THEY CAME FROM

As long as we're reviewing, here's a review of the basic, traditional wedding vows. In the classic, traditional Christian wedding vows, the Clergy person recites:

> *"Dearly beloved, we are gathered together here in the sight of God, and in the face of this congregation, to join together this man and this woman in holy matrimony."*

Then, the Clergy asks the following questions:

> *"Do you, _____, take _____, to be your lawfully wedded wife/husband, to have and to hold, from this day forward, for better for worse, for richer, for poorer, in sickness and in health, to love and to cherish, forsaking all others, till death do you part?"*

And this is where, "I do," comes in.

Some versions end the vow question instead with, "as long as we both shall live." But this is often changed due to the implication that one left widowed, is not free to remarry.

Some Catholic versions also ask, "Will you accept children lovingly from God, and bring them up according to the law of Christ and his Church?"

The couple can also recite the previous question as a statement, one to the other.

"I, _____, take you_____, to be my lawfully wedded wife/husband..."

Some more conservative versions of the vows have also included, "... to love, cherish and obey, according to God's holy ordinance, and thereto I give thee my troth." But because "obey" was authored into these back when women were viewed as property or servants, in the 16th century, this word has since often been eliminated. Some also ask, "Who gives this woman to be married?" Again, this has often been deleted, depending on the nature of the ceremony and denomination.

Next, while placing the ring on one another's fingers, the betrothed then vow:

"With this ring, I thee wed, with my body I thee worship, and with all my worldly goods I thee endow. In the name of the Father, and of the Son, and of the Holy Spirit." Amen."

These vows that we call Traditional, evolved only slightly from the English Book of Common Prayer, dating back to 1549, with some alterations from 1662.[ii]

There you have it.

They are pretty clear, straightforward, and frankly, profound. But at the same time, they're not necessarily very romantic or emotional. Which brings us to today's proclivity for writing original vows, whether by the minister (or Officiant), or the couple.

While the classic vows may tug on your sense of tradition, there is real wisdom in writing one's own vows. The experience of doing it offers couples a chance to think about what their marriage means to them.

The thought it takes to write or consider alternative vows, can create even more contemplation about the marriage itself.

The Most Important Part – Ask Your Officiant

Though original, or self-composed vows are extremely common today, it's imperative that you ask your ceremony Officiant about their parameters for original vows, or meeting any religious requirements if that's the case with your wedding. You will also want to verify that they meet with your Officiant's approval long before the big day, because he or she will be sealing the ceremony.

SAMPLE VOWS
36 UNIQUE EXAMPLES

Consider a few original vows that follow. They can become as religious or non-religious as a couple desires, with just a few alterations. They can be personalized in lots of ways. Some include differing lines for bride and groom; some would be matched.

And if these aren't a perfect fit for your wedding, we'll move into 10 methods to help you write entirely original vows, specifically for you, in later chapters.

#1 *I Recognized You*

I hardly need to vow.
The vow was made by our meeting.
I recognized you.
I believed in you from that first encounter.
I believed in fate for the first time after meeting you.
Because all else afterwards just made sense, when it came to you and I as a pair.
I feel like the vow was made in some other place, and finding you only makes it real in this one.
So here I am. (With this ring), I give you all of me, in front of this community.
To love, to cherish. To be bound together in all the earthly ways that heaven intended for us all along.
I will love you always. I have loved you always.

#2. *Actions Speak*

Today, I promise to be your loving husband/wife.
I vow to be your strength, you companion, and your true love.
But today, I also promise to do much to make this vow remembered as the years go by...
I promise to appreciate all you do, and to tell you so often.
I promise to tell you what you mean to me.
I promise to always kiss you goodnight, and never go to bed without resolving a hurt.
I promise to make time for just the two of us, no matter how hectic life gets.
I promise to hold your heart as my most valued possession, because today I honor that you've given it to me.
And because now our hearts belong to each other, I will cherish yours, and remember my promises with this ring, as symbol of everything I've said.

#3 My Love, My Friend

You are my most cherished friend, my dearest friend, and my truest friend.

Today we become the most committed of friends.

Though we're imperfect, our love is perfectly steadfast.

Though the world gives us trials, my vow to you, is to give us devotion,

and to care for our marriage as dearly as I care for myself.

It is not to put you above me, or below me, but to make "us" the first priority.

You are the match for me that I always longed for.

You are my dream come true.

I promise to honor you for this, all the days of my life.

#4 A Renewal Vow

I give you to you today, myself...older, wiser and even more true to you and I, than I was the first time I made this promise.

_____, you have been the charm in my life that makes my experiences more whole, more joyous and more rewarding. For this and for you, I am truly grateful. My heart could burst from sheer thankfulness.

I am so glad to have married you.

You double my comfort and divide my grief.

I vow again, to love you all the days of my life.

The best is yet to come.

#5. *Alternative Renewal Vow*

My dearly beloved, you are my rock, my protector, my caretaker and my friend. Despite our ups and downs, you are always, my favorite person.
I think you're everything a husband ought to be, and I'm I would marry you over and over again. And today, I am. I vow to love you, forever and ever.

You are my sweetheart, my muse, my caretaker and my better half. Despite any bumps life brings us, you are always, my favorite person.
You are more than I could ever dream of a wife being. And now, I give thanks that I can make this vow to love you always, once again. And I am. With this ring, I vow to love you, forever and always.

#6 Inter-Faith Vows

I promise to wipe away tears with laughter;
to tend to your wounds and uplift your spirit.
I promise to love you, keep you, be faithful to you,
and value you.
I promise to honor your heritage, and your
family's,
And to love without exclusion, as God does.
Today, we let God's amazing grace show itself in
us, and receive the gift of love, which blossomed
when God put us in each other's life.
I give myself to our sacred union, completely
joyously and forever.

For a couple who marries a second time:

#7. Re-Marriage Vows

"Second Chances"

_____ I am so grateful for second chances. I celebrate our reunion, as one that brings past and future together. For you and I, there is only permanence; a bond that I recommit to, now and forevermore. Today with joy and gratitude, I vow to be your ever-loving wife.

_____ here we are, lucky and blessed, to enjoy the grace of a new beginning. You are my home, and you always will be. I vow to love, honor and cherish you, all the days of my life, as your devoted husband.

#8 *We Over I*

I promise to comfort you in times of struggle
I promise to rejoice with you in times of joy.
I promise to remember to laugh, when I feel like holding a grudge.
I promise to remember that not everything is important; but I promise to realize that little things can be.
I promise to love you with patience, compassion and appreciation for exactly the person you are.
Today, we become a family.
Today, I vow that "we" are more important than "I". That "us" is stronger than "me".
With this ring, I promise to do what's best for us in every way I can. And I promise to love, honor and be faithful to our union, for the rest of my life.

#9 Until I Met You

Until I met you I only suspected what real love was.
I knew what a crush was.
I knew disappointment.
I knew hope.
But now I know certainty.
I am certain of our permanence.
I am certain. I am steadfast.
And I am utterly honored to say I'm now you're wife/husband.
Take this ring as a symbol of my vow, to be as certain of this dedication to you – forevermore -- as I am today.   And thank you for giving me the experience of real love. I will protect and honor that love, always.

*10 You Surprise Me

Two years ago, I met a man who surprised me. He surprised me because I didn't think there was anyone who would love me truly, the way I always dreamed it could be. I have been surprised ever since, by how happy I have been.

I promise to keep surprising you, with devotion, affection, forgiveness, laughter, courage and kindness all the days of my life.

With this ring, I ____, take you_____ to be my lawfully wedding husband/wife.

#11 All I Ever Wanted

I have all that I have ever wanted. But I promise to keep growing anyway, to dream bigger dreams with you, to have and to hold you as we achieve and grow and gain and lose, as life presses on. I vow to remember, that in sickness and in health, that for better or worse, and for richer and poorer, no matter what comes and goes, that if I have you, I still have all I ever wanted: Love.

#12. *It's About Us Now*

A friend once asked me why I wanted to get married. I said, because "I'm over me." I knew I was ready to share life, and to make it about us...and I hadn't even met you yet.

Knowing you has convinced me this was the wisest leap of faith I've ever made... to go looking for you so that id be ready when you showed up.

I'm so happy. Your love improves my happiness and abates misery, by doubling my joys and dividing my grief. * I promise to make it about "us" forever.

#13. Gratitude

Thank you for feeling everything that I felt.
Thank you for knowing that we were special.
Thank you for the faith that we belong together.
Thank you for loving me.
I can hardly believe you do.
You make me so happy.
You make me so proud.
You make me so honored that you'll spend your life with me.
With this ring, I promise to do my very best to honor you, by feeling this gratitude for the rest of my life. I take you as my lawfully wedded husband/wife.

* from the renowned quote of English writer, Joseph Addison

#14. Funny Vows
"To Love Your Sense of Humor Too"

____, *With this ring, I thee wed. I promise to love, honor and cherish you, now and forever.*

I promise not to ask if I look fat, more than once per month.

I promise to consult with you for any expenditure over $200, unless it's for surprise gift tickets to the ____game.

I promise to squeeze the toothpaste from the bottom of the tube... from today on,

I promise to appreciate your sense of humor, even if I have to do a fake laugh sometimes.

_____, *With this ring, I thee wed. I promise to love, honor and cherish you all the days of my life. Also, I promise to call if I'm more than 10 minutes late.*

I promise never to buy you a small appliance as a romantic gift.

I promise tell you, you look thin, more than once per month.

I promise to always use a coaster,

And I promise to appreciate your sense of humor, even if I have to explain it to other people sometimes.

15. *"Your Most Loyal Companion"*

_____, I'm so happy to be marrying you. You have been my strength, my hero, and my jester all in one man. I promise to love, respect and honor you, all the days of my life. To face life's challenges together; to be slow to anger, and quick to laugh, and to notice your strengths and your victories, and be your most loyal companion...forever.

_____ you make me want to be a better man, because you're such a good woman. I promise to put our needs ahead of my own, and to make our home and family my biggest priority; without question. I promise to love, honor and cherish you forever.

16. "Because You're Mine, I'm at Peace."

____, you have brought a peace to me I didn't know before. I am at peace...the kind of peace that comes from confidence and security, and from knowing you love me. I vow now to do everything I can, to always fill you with the same peace, the same knowing that I love you steadfastly too.
With this ring, I vow it solemnly; that you are my everlasting love, no matter what.

_____, you have brought me the peace that allows joy. I have a confidence in our love I've never known, and that makes me steadfast and glad. I promise you now and always, that my love for you will be unwavering and permanent, no matter what life brings. With this ring, I promise you all of myself, forever.

17. *"Thank You for Loving Me"*

_____, *Thank you for loving me. I will spend my whole life devoted to our partnership, and to showing you and telling you, how much I love you, too. Take this ring as a symbol of my faith in you, and my conviction that life is better with us together. Every time you look at it, please remember my love and commitment.*

_____, *Thank you for loving me. I will spend all my life faithful and steadfast that our union is blessed, and I will do my utmost to show you how important you are to me. Take this ring as a symbol of my faith in you, and my conviction that life is better with us together. Every time you look at it, please remember my love and commitment.*

18. "When You Look At This Ring"

_____, I vow to you today, to love, honor and cherish you, and to be your best friend, lover, confidante and partner.

Take this ring and when you look at it, remember that I will stand by you forever, in sickness and in health, for richer for poorer, come what may; you've got a true wife in me.

_____, I vow to you today, to love, honor and cherish you, and to be your best friend, lover, confidante and partner.

Take this ring and when you look at it, always remember that I will stand by you forever, in sickness and in health, for richer for poorer...come what may - you have a true husband in me.

19. "My Promise Is Sacred"

_____, my promise today is sacred. I vow to love, honor, trust and cherish you, in sickness and in health, whether we are rich or poor and through all the ups and downs in between that a life lived fully, will surely bring us. I pledge today to be your faithful wife and to love you fully, for as long as I live.

_____, my promise today is sacred. I vow to love, honor, trust and cherish you; in sickness and in health, whether we are rich or poor, and through all the ups and downs in between, that a life lived fully, will surely bring us. I pledge today, to be your faithful husband and to love you fully, for as long as I live.

20. "You Are My Home"

_____, I'm overjoyed to marry you. I know that I'm at home when we're together. I love you. I'm proud to call you my husband. And today, I vow to be yours, faithfully, forever.

_____, I'm so happy to marry you. I know that you are my true companion. I love you. I'm proud to call you my wife. And today, I vow to be yours, faithfully, forever.

21. "It Was Just A Matter of Time'

_____, it's hard to imagine that I was ever looking for you, because now that you're here, I can see it was all just a matter of time. You were always my destiny, and I'm thrilled to be living it. Take this ring, as a symbol of time and eternity, and how I have been yours since before we even met. I vow to honor, love and keep you, in sickness and in health, for richer for poorer, and for all time._

_____, I always thought it might be scary to get married, but with you, it's easy. I can see you were my destiny. You make me always want to be someone you're proud of. Take this ring, as a symbol of time and eternity, and how I have been yours since before we event met. I vow to love, cherish and honor you, for better or for worse, and for all time._

22. "So Easy To Say, I Do"

_____, with you, it's easy to see myself with one person, for my whole life.
I've always known you were right for me, and that's what makes it easy. I'm ready to be the best wife I can be, to love you unconditionally, and always. Take this ring, and know - that I know - our marriage, is right, and our partnership, forever.

_____, with you, it's easy to say, "I do." It's easy to take a step I couldn't imagine before I met you...because you are my other half. You are my home. You are where everything is all right. Take this ring, and know - that I know - our marriage, is right, and our life together, forever.

23. "To Have And To Hold"

_____, from this day forward, I am your wife. I take you to have and to hold, to rely on and to be steadfast for, to be faithful to, and to have trust in.

This ring is a circle; a symbol of the love that has no beginning and no end, but always was and is. With this ring, I wed my best friend and my love.

_____, from this day forward, I am your husband. I take you to have and to hold, to rely on and to be steadfast for, to be faithful to, and to have faith in.

This ring is a circle; a symbol of the love that has no beginning and no end, but always was and is. With this ring, I wed my best friend and my love.

24. "To Be Your Sweetheart Too"

_____, today, I vow to marry you, to be yours faithfully, through every joy and challenge of life. But today, I also promise to be more - to be your wife - and to be your sweetheart too. Because I never want to lose that sense of romance, excitement, and trust in you that we had in the beginning.

Take this ring, both as a symbol of the love that is beyond time, and of my own commitment to show you my respect, trust and admiration forever.

_____, today, I vow to marry you, to be yours faithfully, through every joy and challenge of life. But today, I also promise to be more - to be your husband - and to always be your hero too. Because I never want to lose that sense of romance, excitement, and trust in you that we had in the beginning.

Take this ring, both as a symbol of the love that is beyond time, and of my own commitment to show you my respect, trust, and admiration forever.

25. "My Home Is Where You Are"

Today, I take you _____, to be my husband. To quote a song, "I need you in my house, because you're my home." I take you to be my lawfully wedded husband, in good times and in bad. I promise to make love our life's foundation. Take this ring, and know that from this day forward, home is wherever you are.

I take you _____, to be my wife. To love and to cherish, and to build my home with, no matter where we are. In good times and in bad, I promise love. Take this ring, and know that from this day forward, home is wherever you are.

26. "You Get Me"

_____, you don't complete me; I'm complete alone.

You get me. That's more important.

I'm so at peace and happy with you. Today, I take you to be my husband, to have and to hold, to honor, to cherish, to value... and to get. I vow to honor and respect you and be your wife, so long as we both shall live. I get that.

_____, you're not my better half, you're my other whole. And you get me.

I'm so proud to marry you today, and I'm so confident in making a lifelong vow to you, that I will love you, cherish you, value you...and I will honor and keep you and to be your loving husband, so long as we both shall live. I get that.

27. "You're My Gravity"

_____, to quote a song... you are my gravity. My life has a center when we're together. But in your love, I am both grounded and safe, and free and adventurous.

Today, I vow to you _____, to be your grounding, you wife, your companion, your nurturer, and your friend. I will love you and keep you so long as we both shall live.

_____, you're my compass. I'll never be lost with us in partnership. You give me a give me a starting point for everything. I vow to step forward with you in every way, for every dream we share, and for every adventure we undertake. I will love you and keep you and cherish you, for the rest of our lives.

28. "A Love That's Beyond Me"

_____, this love is beyond me, and this gives me comfort. I know that together, we are better and happier than apart. I didn't so much choose to love you, as I surrendered to it - to a greater calling in our union.

Take this ring, and know that I vow to be your loving wife; to honor and keep you, in sickness and in health, for richer and poorer, till death do us part.

_____, this love is bigger than I ever imagined, and that's what makes it easy to say _I Do_. I know that together, we are happy and comforted, and joyous and grateful for our love.

Take this ring, and know that I vow to be your loving husband; to honor and keep you, in sickness and in health, for richer and poorer, till death do us part.

29. "My Crush"

I promise never to lose my crush entirely. I promise to let my heart leap a little when I see you after an absence, just like it did in the beginning.
I promise to see the past as cherished, the future as blessed, and to never forget how I love you, in each present day.
I promise to see your beauty from the inside out.
I promise to appreciate your love and companionship.

I promise to still let myself get excited to see you, and to go out of our way to spend romantic time together.
I promise to see the past as cherished, the future as blessed, and to always honor that I love you, in the present.
I promise that no matter how much the practicalities and stresses of life arise, I will always maintain a little bit of that crush I've had on you.

30. From, "To Be One With Each Other" by George Eliot

_____, today, I take you to be my wedded husband.
We are joined together to strengthen each other in all labor
to minister to each other in all sorrow,
to share with each other in all gladness,
and to be one with each other in the silent,
unspoken memories, we will create.

_____, today, I take you to be my wedded wife.
We are joined together to strengthen each other in all labor,
to minister to each other in all sorrow,
to share with each other in all gladness,
and to be one with each other in the silent,
unspoken memories, we have yet to create.
What greater thing is there for two human souls?

31. From "To My Dear and Loving Husband" by Anne Bradstreet

If ever two were one, then surely we.
If ever man were lov'd by wife, then thee.
If ever wife was happy in a man,
Compare with me, ye women, if you can.
I prize thy love more than whole Mines of gold,
Or all the riches that the East doth hold.
_____, I vow to be your lawfully wedded wife.
You make me happy, and I value our love more
than riches. So...till death do us part, in sickness
and in health, and for richer for poorer, I am
yours, and I am happy for it.

My love is such that Rivers cannot quench,
Nor ought but love from thee give recompense.
Thy love is such I can in no way repay;
The heavens reward thee manifold I pray.
Then while we live, in love lets so persevere,
That when we live no more, we may live ever.
_____ I vow to be your lawfully wedded husband.
You are my reward, and I value your love more
than anything. It will persevere, till death do us
part, in sickness and in health, and for richer or
poorer. I am yours, I am happy for it.

32. From "Love Is A Great Thing" by Thomas a Kempis

From Thomas Kempis: Love is able to undertake all things...where he who does not love would faint and lie down. Your love makes me stronger, and I vow today to be your strength.

_____, today I promise to love you always, so that we'll have the strength to undertake all things as man and wife. Know this ring is a reminder of my vow, and my steadfast love, till death do us part.

_____, today I promise to love you always, so that we'll have the strength to undertake all things as man and wife. Know this rings is a reminder of my vow, and my steadfast love, till death us do part.

33. "I Am Devoted"

I am so touched, so happy that words can hardly express it. _____, I adore you, I admire you, and I vow today to do so for all of my days. Thank you for loving me.

With this ring, always remember that I am steadfast in love, and my heart is devoted, come what may... wealth or health or circumstance of any kind, I am always devoted.

_____, I am yours, from this day forward, as husband and wife. You give me comfort, joy and inspiration, and I vow today that I will love you for all of my days.

With this ring, always remember that I am steadfast in my love and commitment, and I am devoted, come what may...wealth or health or circumstance of any kind. I am always devoted.

34. "I've Never Been So Sure"

_____, I've never been so happy as I am with you, and knowing you love me. I am my best self around you. You make me want to grow in every way, because I admire you so.
Take this ring, as a symbol of my love, my hope and my promise, to be a loving, faithful and loyal wife to you, for as long as we both shall live.

_____, I've known we were to be together from the very beginning. I'm happiest with you, and sure our union is sacred and true. You make me want to be the best man I can be, because you're such a good woman. Take this ring, as a symbol of my love, my hope and my promise, to be a loving, faithful and loyal husband to you, for as long as we both shall live.

35. "I See You"

_____, I don't just love you, I know you. And I see all that you do and who you are. I see your hard work, I see your devotion, I see your hopes and your uniqueness, and for how much I value all that I see, I'm marrying you.

   With this ring, I promise to love, honor and keep you, to be your confidante and your partner, in sickness and in health, for richer for poorer...I will always see you for who you are, my true love.

_____, I don't just love you, I recognize you. I recognize your heart, your kindness, your diligence, your faithfulness, I see your hopes and your grace, and for all that I recognize in you, I'm marrying you.

   With this ring, I promise to love, honor and keep you, to be your hero and your friend, in sickness and in health, for richer or for poorer...I will always recognize that you are my true love.

36. "Everything"

I promise ...everything that unites us in love, always.

I promise to be your wife... to make us the first priority, to honor and understand you, to inspire and listen, to be your safe place.

With this ring, I pledge my devotion and my faith in you, my faithfulness to you, and my faith in the grace that brought us together. Know that I am yours, as is everything I have, till death do us part.

TEN GUIDES
FOR WRITING YOUR OWN
WEDDING VOWS

And 15 additional samples along the way.

Now we'll peruse a variety of methods and inspirations to write your own wedding vows, with fourteen more samples following each.

The good news is, vows aren't terribly long. If you consider the length of the traditional vows, it's really only a few sentences or paragraphs at best. You're not writing the great American novel.

Take out a pen and paper, make notes in your eBook reader, or even open a text-only document to make notes within that, while you read along through this book.

Each Guide concludes with yet another sample vow, demonstrating that particular technique.

GUIDE ONE:
USE THESE INSPIRATIONAL QUESTIONS

Take just a moment, to contemplate each question, and jot down a few words in response to the particular questions that spark a response in you -- not a paragraph, just a note, or some words to jog your memory.

Important Points: If some questions just don't spark an immediate or clear answer – no worries -- simply move on to one that does! You're only looking for 1-3 of these questions to really get you going.

Vows are not that long, after all, so keep it brief and easy.

a) How did you meet? What do you remember about the first time you met?

Little did you know then, that ____?

b) When were you interested in him/her, if it was not at your first meeting?

c) When did you know you loved him/her?

d) What are three qualities you like best about your fiancé?

f) What do you see in him/her that no one else sees, or sees as clearly as you do?

g) Why do you love him/her?

h) What are three hopes you have for the future, big or small?

i) What good things does he/she bring out in you?

k) How are you better as a couple than as individuals?

l) How does his/her love make you feel in general?

m) How does he/she make you feel about yourself?

n) What hopes does he/she bring out in you?

o) Before meeting him/her, what did you expect of marriage?

p) What do you promise to keep doing for him/her?

q) What do you promise to keep feeling for him/her?

r) What is holy, spiritual, or eternal about this union for you?

s) What kind of vow would you love to hear from your fiancé? Write out what you would love to hear promised, *specifically to you.*

Is that vow, what you would like to say to him/her?

Many people find that just doing this exercise above -- the Q &A -- completely inspires them to jump into writing their own vows.

But if you're still not sure, try this.

Take your three most emotionally stirring answers, and turn them into the beginning, middle and end of your vow!

An example, starting with sample answers:

a) He believes in me. He think I can achieve even more than I do, but in a faithful, not condescending way. He makes me dream.

i) He makes me laugh, and he makes me feel like I'm special. This makes me want to be the best person I can be.

k) Everyday, I think about the future now. And I know that I have a partner who has my best interest at heart. I've never really had that before.

Sample Vow #37 follows, which could be developed from these answers:

> _____, before I met you, I had dreams. But with you, I know the joy of dreaming even bigger. I've known you were a special person from the first days I met you, and you make me want to be a better person in absolutely every way.
>
> I promise that I will always remember and honor the way I feel about you now, all the days of my life. I promise you my unending love, unwavering loyalty... and to always dream with you.

Take one of the ideas that most resonates with you, (like dreams) and make it both the opening, and the closing. In other words, bring it back around, and your vow will feel "well written."

GUIDE TWO:
TAKE THE TRADITIONAL VOWS AND SPIN THEM

If you're a person of few words, use part of the traditional vows, and re-write just one portion of them. That's only a sentence or two for you to write.

Opening:

> *"Dearly beloved, we are gathered together here in the sight of God, and in the face of this congregation, to join together this man and this woman in holy matrimony."*

Then, the Clergy asks the following questions, or bride/groom speak this part:

"Do you, _____, take _____, to be your lawfully wedded wife/husband, to have and to hold, from this day forward, for better for worse, for richer, for poorer, in sickness and in health, to love and to cherish, forsaking all others, till death do you part?"

White putting the ring on:

"With this ring, I thee wed, with my body I thee worship, and with all my worldly goods I thee endow. In the name of the Father, and of the Son, and of the Holy Spirit." Amen."

You can use the traditional question, then for the ring placement, re-write what the ring means to you.

An example of a resulting, custom ending, #38:

"Let this ring be a symbol of my unending promise; that I am bound to you happily. That I will love you, honor you, uphold you and support you as my love and my treasure. "

Or write your own question or promise, and use the Traditional version of the ring placement instead.

What are three things you promise?

To love you
To cherish you
To be by your side
To remember this day forever
To appreciate you
To never take a day for granted
To be faithful to you
To journey with you as a loving partner
To give myself to you
To be grateful for our union
To enjoy the good times and the bad
To love you through equally through both the joys
and challenges of life
To believe in you
To be your greatest believer
To be your greatest admirer
To have and to hold you
To honor you

An example of your own vow promise might be vow
example #39:

I_____, take you_____ to be my
loving husband/wife. I promise to love you, be
faithful to you...to be your greatest supporter. And
I give myself to you with my whole heart, forever
grateful for the life we live together.

You may follow with the traditional ring pledge:

"With this ring, I thee wed, with my body I
thee worship, and with all my worldly goods I

thee endow. In the name of the Father, and of the Son, and of the Holy Spirit." Amen."

Either way, you've added a simple, custom touch to your ceremony.

GUIDE THREE:
HARNESS SOME INSPIRATION FROM HOLLYWOOD

Great movie and TV romances are inspiring. We'll take a moment now to comment on some great lines from Hollywood.

Sometimes, a character's proclamation can provide the foundation for a promise of your own, or the launching point for thinking up a personal vow that charms you.

Review the scenes in their entirety, because for copyright reasons, they're only listed here in part for commentary.

From, *When Harry Met Sally* ©1989 MGM:

> *"I love that you get cold when it's seventy-one degrees out. I love that it takes you an hour and a half to order a sandwich. I love that you get a little crinkle in your nose when you're looking at me like I'm nuts. I love that after I spend the day with you, I can still smell your perfume on my clothes. And I love that you are the last person I want to talk to before I go to sleep at night. And it's not because I'm lonely, and it's not because it's New Year's Eve. I came here tonight because when you realize you want to spend the rest of your life with somebody, you want the rest of your life to start as soon as possible."*

Wow. Don't you just wish Harry would make that phenomenal speech his wedding vow to Sally? How much better does it get than that?

Is your fiancé the last person you want to talk to before you go to sleep? Do you want the rest of your life to start as soon as possible? Do you love the things that should be annoying? Are you committed to still seeing your fiancé's habits as charming years from now? I doubt Universal would sue you for giving this speech verbatim in a little old wedding. Screenwriter Nora Ephron might just be proud.

From, *Bull Durham* ©1988 MGM Studios:

> *"Well, I believe in the soul, the c*&#, the p*#%#@, the small of a woman's back, the hanging curve ball, high fiber, good scotch, that the novels of Susan Sontag are self-indulgent overrated...I believe Lee Harvey Oswald acted alone. I believe there ought to be a constitutional amendment outlawing Astroturf and the designated hitter. I believe in the sweet spot, soft core pornography, opening your presents Christmas morning rather than Christmas Even and I believe in long, slow, deep, soft, wet kisses that last three days."*

Now, while we're in no way suggesting foul language for a wedding, there are certainly ideas in all of us that can stir us up with this kind of passion. What do you believe in? Go ahead and pretend to be Crash Davis for a moment. If he were speaking about your fiancé' and what he believes about your marriage, what would he say? It's a macho kind of way to say things that matter, isn't it?

From, *Knotting Hill* © 1999 Universal Studios:

> *"...Don't forget I'm just a girl, standing in front of a boy, asking him to love her.*

Are some vows too flowery? If you could put it simply like this, how would you?

From Sleepless In Seattle © 1993 TriStar Pictures:

> *"It was a million tiny little things that,
> when you added them all up, they meant
> we were supposed to be together...and I
> knew it. I knew it the very first time I
> touched her. It was like coming home, only
> to no home I'd ever known. I was just
> taking her hand to help her out of a car and
> I knew."*

As long as we're commenting on Nora Ephron's brilliance, let's do it twice. If only she could write everyone's wedding vows... What are the million tiny things that mean you're supposed to be together? Or maybe, what are three of them? When did you "know"?

From The Notebook © 2004 New Line Cinema:

> *"That's my sweetheart in
> there. Wherever she is, that's
> where my home is."*

Go review the entire scene -- heck -- the whole movie. Jot down some notes. You may want to say some things this simply. Is a metaphor the way to describe your betrothed?

From The Princess Bride © 1997 MGM:

> *"That day, she was amazed to discover that when he was saying, "As you wish," what he really meant was, "I love you." And even more amazing was the day she realized she truly loved him back. "*

So when did you know you loved your fiancé? Were they doing or saying something other than "I love you" which really meant the same thing?

From a post-it-note in Grey's Anatomy ©2010 ABC Television Season 5:

> *"...to love each other, even when we hate each other. No running ever; nobody walks out no matter what happens. Take care when old, senile, smelly."*

If you had to fit your vows on a post-it note, what would they be?

Speaking of simple...
<u>From As Good As It Gets © 1997 TriStar Pictures:</u>

"You make me want to be a better man."

And here's a more complicated version:

> *"I might be the only one who appreciates how amazing you are in every single thing that you do, and...how you say what you mean, and how you almost always mean something that's all about being straight and good. I think most people miss that about you, and I watch them, wondering how they can watch you bring their food and clear their tables and never get that they just met the greatest woman alive. And the fact that I get it makes me feel good, about me."* From As Good As It Gets © 1997 TriStar Pictures

Use these thoughts to ask yourself, what do you see in your betrothed that maybe no one else does?

<u>From Braveheart ©1995 Paramount Studios:</u>

"...I will love you my whole life. You and no other."

So simple. You can't beat simple if it's right. How would you write a vow like this? Challenge yourself to write a vow in 12 words or less and see if you don't love it.

From *Friends*, Monica & Chandler's Wedding ©
2001 Warner Bros Television:

> *"Three years ago, at another wedding, I*
> *turned to a friend for comfort. And instead,*
> *I found everything that I'd ever been*
> *looking for my whole life. And now, here*
> *we are with our future before us, and I only*
> *want to spend it with you, my prince, my*
> *soul mate, my friend."*

How did you meet? Does it deserve mention in your
vows?

And just to illustrate the inspiration, here's an
example of how these kinds of speeches might
inspire a different wedding vow in sample vow #40:

> *"Three years ago, I thought I never wanted*
> *to get married. And then I met my match,*
> *and all the stories I told myself, changed. I*
> *believe in marriage, because I believe in*
> *you, and in us.*
>
> *You make me want to be the best man I can*
> *be. The fact that I recognize how special*
> *you are, makes me feel special.*
>
> *You're my love, my soul mate and my*
> *friend. And I want to start the rest of my*
> *life as your husband, as soon as possible."*

All the Previous Film & TV Productions are
available for download in full from Amazon.

GUIDE FOUR:
USE CLASSIC POETRY AS A
FOUNDATION

So maybe you're not a poet. That's OK. Other people are. These poems are in the public domain, so we can print them fully, unlike entire movie scripts.

And whether you use these poems exactly, use excerpts, or use them as launching points, they're gorgeous. You can use just a few lines of a favorite. Either way, you can't go wrong with a classic.

"Believe Me, If All Those Endearing Young Charms..."
By Thomas Moore 1779-1852

Believe me, if all those endearing young charms,
Which I gaze on so fondly today,
Were to change by tomorrow, and fleet in my
arms,
Like fairy-gifts fading away,

Though wouldst still be adored, as this moment
thou art,
Let they loveliness fade as it will,
And around the dear ruin each wish of my heart
Would entwine itself verdantly still.

It is not while beauty and youth are thine own,
And thy cheeks unprofaned by a tear
That the fervor and faith of a soul can be known,
To which time will but make thee more dear;

No, the heart that has truly loved never forgets,
But as truly loves on to the close,
As the sunflower turns on her god, when he sets,
The same look which she turned when he rose.

This is truly a gorgeous poem about enduring love, and feeling it long after beauty and youth fade.

If Thou Must Love Me
By Elizabeth Barrett Browning 1806-1861

If thou must love me, let it be for naught
Except for love's sake only. Do not say
"I love her for her smile her look her way
Of speaking gently, for a trick of thought
That falls in well with mine, and certes brought
A sense of ease on such a day:
For these things in themselves, Beloved, may
Be changed or change for thee, and love, so
wrought,
May be unwrought so. Neither love me for
Thine own dear pity's wiping my cheek dry,
A creature might forget to weep, who bore
Thy comfort long, and lose they love thereby!
But love me for love's sake, that evermore
Thou mayst love on, through love's eternity.

To love with a child's faith?
That's a beautiful idea that might belong in a
wedding vow.

"How Do I Love Thee?"
by Elizabeth Barrett Browning

How do I love thee? Let me count the ways.
I love thee to the depth and breadth and height
My soul can reach, when feeling out of sight
For the ends of Being and ideal Grace.

I love thee to the level of everyday's
Most quiet need, by sun and candlelight.
I love thee freely, as men strive for Right;
I love thee purely, as they turn from Praise.

I love thee with the passion put to use
In my old griefs, and with my childhood's faith.
I love thee with a love I seemed to lose
With my lost saints, I love thee with the breath,
Smiles, tears, of all my life! and, if God choose,
I shall but love thee better after death.

This poem is about the difference between love for another, and love simply to please oneself. The first four lines might make a lovely foundation of a wedding vow.

The Clod and the Pebble
by William Blake (1757-1827)

Love seeketh not Itself to please,
Nor for itself hath any care;
But for another gives its ease,
And builds a Heaven in Hells despair.

So sang a little Clod of Clay,
Trodden with the cattle's feet;
But a Pebble of the brook,
Warbled out these metres meet.

Love seeketh only Self to please,
To bind another to its delight:
Joys in another's loss of ease,
And builds a Hell in Heavens despite.

And if you chose not to use any lines of poetry precisely, here's an example of how this classic poetry might inspire a unique wedding vow,

Sample #41:

> "_____, today I stand to take you as my husband/wife.
>
> And if all your endearing charms were to fade by tomorrow, I would still love you. Time will only make you more dear to me.
>
> I love you freely, and with a child's purity of faith.
>
> I love you for love's sake, and know that I'll be closer to heaven - even in our most trying days - than I would ever have been without you."

Note: For many more poetry and classical writings, see *50 Unique Wedding Readings*, also available in paperback or eBook form.

GUIDE FIVE:
USE BIBLE VERSES AS A
FOUNDATION

While anyone who's ever attended a Christian wedding is no doubt familiar with the popular Corinthians reading ... imagine taking just a portion of it to use, not as a reading, but to use as your vow.

Sample Vow #42 Inspired by Corinthians 13:7

"Love bears all things, believes all things, hopes all things, endures all things. This is the love, I vow to you; to bear, believe, hope, and endure. As long as I live, I vow to love you. And to be at your side, for all things, forever more."

More sample vow #42 Inspired by Corinthians 13:8

"Love never ends. As for prophecies, they will pass away; as for tongues, they will cease; as for knowledge, it will pass away. But my love for you is ever-lasting."

I promise not to be self-seeking, to not easily anger, to keep no record of wrongs, to always protect, trust, hope and persevere with you, my husband/wife.

Other verses you might find inspirational:

"A faithful friend is the medicine of life."
- Ecclesiasticus 6:16

"I will betroth you to me forever. I will betroth you to me in righteousness and in justice, in steadfast love and in mercy. I will betroth you to me in faithfulness."
- Hosea 2:19

GUIDE SIX:
GET THEE TO A BOOK OF SHAKESPEARE

If you're going to use the words of a professional, why not use the best? Shakespeare's written more successfully about love, than anyone.

Here are three examples, to lift from or inspire.

From *Romeo & Juliet:*
"My bounty is as boundless as the sea,
My love as deep; the more I give to thee,
The more I have for both are infinite."

This basically says, my love is so great, that the more I give, the more I have.

Sonnet 116:

Let me not to the marriage of true minds
admit impediments. Love is not love
which alters when it alteration finds,
or bends with the remover to remove:
Oh, no! It is an ever-fixed mark.
That looks on tempests and is never shaken;
it is the star to every wandering bark,
whose worth's unknown, although his height be
taken.
Love's not Time's fool, though rosy lips and cheeks
within his bending sickle's compass come;
love alters not with his brief hours and weeks,
but bears it out even to the edge of doom.
If this be error and upon me proved,
I never writ, nor no man ever loved.

From *Hamlet*:

Doubt thou the stars are fire;
Doubt that the sun doth move;
Doubt truth to be a liar;
But never doubt I love.

This basically says, my love is truer than the stars or the sun, or truth itself.

Get creative if you like. If you do not use a passage directly, you could use the thoughts and meanings behind them to write your own vow.

Here's an example of a vow which utilizes both a verbatim lift of Shakespeare, and an inspiration from him, mixed.

You could say it like this, sample vow #43:

From the heart of Shakespeare:

"Doubt thou the stars are fire;
Doubt that the sun doth move;
Doubt truth to be a liar,
But never doubt I love.

My love for you is truer than truth itself.
And I know it's true, because with you? The
more love I give, the more I have. I promise
you my love is unending and
unwavering...an ever-fixed mark, and it
will never be shaken. "

GUIDE SEVEN:
HOW TO WRITE FUNNY VOWS

The definition of funny" has been described as something that generates recognition and surprise. That basically means, truth in an unexpected package.

So here's the trick to writing funny: be truthful.

We're not saying that straight vows aren't truthful, but there's a special ring of recognition is something that's *comically* true.

Go back to your list of answers to the inspiring questions, from Chapter 1. If you truly love, it's very likely that something from that list rings as funny.

If not, ask yourself (and your fiancé') the following questions:

1. What are the three most likely daily-life-annoyances we'll face?

2. What day-to-day, pragmatic things should we agree on and haven't stated?

3. What are your three biggest weaknesses/bad habits?

With these, you'll have some truth to work with.

Now for the surprise part.

It is a wedding, not a roast, so humor must be gentle or self-deprecating. That means you only make yourself the butt of a joke, otherwise you come off as a heel!

Perhaps your vows are formal and lovely, with just a touch of humor, using the answers to your questions.

It might go something like this, sample vow #44:

> *"I _____, take _____, to be my lawfully wedded wife/husband, to have and to hold, for better for worse, for richer, for poorer, in sickness and in health, to love and to cherish, till death do us part.*
>
> *To this end, I also promise:*

HIS:

No TV in the bedroom

I will call if I'm running late.

If I become a snorer, I promise to seek treatment.

HERS:

To this end, I also promise:

Only flip-top, permanently-attached toothpaste caps.

No purchases above $100 without mutual agreement ahead of time, except for shoes.

No mom jeans, even when I'm a mom.

TOGETHER:

And positively, no Facebooking old relationships, ever.

RING EXCHANGE:

With this ring, I thee wed. Let it be a symbol of my unwavering love, and good humor, always.

You get the idea.

Here are a few more lines to stoke the creative fire. Just avoid infernos in wedding vows, OK?

I vow, no socks with sandals anymore.

I promise never to ask if an outfit makes me look fat.

I promise to stop leaving my wallet in the car.

I promise to do the dishes half the time.

I promise never to wear a clip on tie.

I promise to stop leaving my shoes everywhere in the house. And if I don't, you're allowed to bug me about it.

I promise weekly date nights out of the house, no matter what. Netflix doesn't count.

I promise to tell you if I get a ticket.

I promise to be patient and understanding if you ever get a ticket again.

I promise to remember my sense of humor, always.

The most important point: keep the funny minimal, and light, and get it approved by your Officiant well before the wedding!

Also, as humor is in *the ear of the beholder*, funny vows should be shared ahead of time to be safe. A few peers with exceptional interpersonal skills should even review them as well.

Now for some more truth-telling...

Are you the kind of person whose humor goes over well in social settings? Or do you have a history of offending?

Tread lightly with your humor. There's certainly a place for it, depending on the couple, but get some back-up opinions first.

And remember, self-deprecation is the rule of the day if you're determined to go the funny route.

GUIDE EIGHT:
USE YOUR OFFICIANT'S STANDARD VOWS, AND REQUEST TO CUSTOMIZE THEM

Your Officiant will do doubt have a pre-determined set of vows for the brides and grooms who don't write their own. Ask him or her about this early on, and ask if you may work with those vows, to alter them a bit and make them more personal. Typically, it's allowed, but always ask first.

Here is one example. The Officiant's vow, sample #45:

"We are gathered here now to witness the joining of _____ and _____, who have desired to bond their lives in happy union. Today, they profess to the world, in the company of their loved ones, their intention to devote their lives to one another, and share their life's journey, in mutual love and support.

Their marriage signifies a rebirth of each of these two individuals... as now, halves of a whole. They come together completely, and will leave here, redefined... as holders of a sacred and beautiful pact.

And we are delighted to celebrate it! Will you take one another's hands?

Do you, _____ , with whole heart, take _____ to be your lawfully wedded husband? Knowing there will be love, and there will be challenge, there will be hope, and there will be loss, there will be joy and there will be sadness, and that this, is your sacred vow?

(Repeat after me)
"This ring serves as a symbol of my never ending commitment to you,_____."

Having proclaimed these truths as vow to one another, to the world, and here to your loved ones, I now pronounce you, Husband and Wife.

Who knows? Perhaps you want these vows a little more upbeat. So give it a go. Sample vow #46:

"We are gathered here now to witness the celebration of _____'s and _____'s happy union in marriage. Today, in the company of their loved ones, they share their intention to devote their lives to one another in loving kindness, and with whole-hearted delight.

And we are delighted to celebrate it!

Their marriage signifies a rebirth of each of these two individuals, as now -- halves of a whole. They come together completely, as they make a sacred and beautiful pact.

Take one another's hands.

I, ____ with whole heart, take _____ to be my wedded husband/wife, knowing there will be love and there will be challenge, there will be joys and there will be tests, and despite it all, my love for you, and my vow to our marriage will be unwavering.

Repeat after me as you place the ring: "This ring serves as a symbol of my never ending love and happiness in marrying you."

Having proclaimed these truths as vow to one another, and here to your loved ones, I now pronounce you, Husband and Wife."

Let's say you love a particular passage of poetry, and want to use it...but don't want to re-write vows entirely. Use the Officiant's vows and add your poetry.

Perhaps insert it during the placement of the rings. Sample vow #47:

"In the words of Shakespeare,

> *Doubt thou the stars are fire;*
> *Doubt that the sun doth move;*
> *Doubt truth to be a liar,*
> *But never doubt I love.*

(as you place the ring)

> *"This ring serves as a symbol of my unending love and vow. For as long as I live I am devoted to you."*

If the bottom line is, you like some of your Officiant's vows, but want a little something else? Ask to do a little something else.

GUIDE NINE:
BE INSPIRED BY BUDDHIST, NATIVE AMERICAN OR ALTERNATIVE TRADITIONS

For a ceremony to be "Buddhist" it's not quite the same as western religions. There is no "Pope" of Buddhism, for example, who sanctions what allowed in the religious rites and what isn't. Instead, Buddhism centers on the practices of present-mindedness.

Buddhism has been described as a constant practice of appreciation, kindness and awareness, with the goal of what has been called, spiritual enlightenment, or the alleviation of suffering. It can also be said it's about the inter-connectedness of all things.

This means that creating Buddhist-inspired vows could involve creating statements that reflect Buddhist teachings, of which there are many cornerstones. We'll paraphrase a few of them here:

1. There is a tenant of protecting life
2. Sharing, and taking only what is offered
3. Cultivating kindness and honesty, especially in speech
4. Using sexuality wisely
5. Avoiding anything which clouds perception of the present (chemicals, etc)

The Eightfold Path (also a foundation of Buddhism) includes "right" behavior in eight areas: view, intention, speech, action, livelihood, effort, mindfulness, and concentration.[iii]

Therefore, sample wedding vows inspired by the insights of Buddhism, might center on proclaiming how your lives coexist with all other beings. Or, how you intend kindness and right actions in your partnership.

These ideas can make for meaningful alternative wedding vows or a wedding service, for the non-Christianity inclined.

An example of this kind of inspired vow might be sample vow #48:

"Today, we enter into the commitment of marriage.
I promise to appreciate our lives and the lives we touch together;
I vow to deepen with you, the practices of receptivity, honesty and kindness;
Of listening without judgment,
And of honoring each day and each step we take together, throughout our lives.
Now, with a love as eternal as every moment, I take you to be my loving husband/wife."

There are many sources for additional information about Buddhism[iv], a beautiful faith and practice, even older than Christianity. This overview is in no way meant to over-simplify the religion's tenants, but merely to introduce the reader to a perspective that may speak to the reader in a meaningful way.

Vows Inspired by the Native American, Rite of the 7 Steps

A very simplified description of the Rite, is that the betrothed couple approaches a fire, as loved ones encircle them. The couple takes seven steps together, and makes seven vows as they walk around. They center on responsibility and family, prosperity and growth, devotion and faith, righteousness and charity, joy and happiness, love and friendship, and permanence.[v]

You might make seven statements in your vows, related to these truths. Sample vow #49:

1. I pledge my responsibility to you and our children and our home.
2. You are my joy.
3. I will join you in sacrifice and charity.
4. You make my heart happy.
5. Our love and friendship make us inseparable.
6. I offer myself wholly to you.
7. I will never deceive you and will love you for my lifetime.

GUIDE TEN:
DO SOME MIX 'N MATCH

In this section, we make it really simple. Select the item from each list that resonates with you. Then make those choice(s) from each list, into the foundation of your vows. Put your selections together, and see what you get.

How do you feel about marrying this person?

Happy

Certain

Grateful

Steadfast

Joyful

Proud

Humbled

Fulfilled

Inspired

Excited

Metaphors. What is your mate to you?

Guide, compass

Friend, ally, companion, partner

Treasure, jewel, precious thing

Safe place, your home, your comfort

Inspiration, motivation, fire

My destiny, my hope, my magic

I promise to:

Love

Cherish

Be there for you

Listen

Learn

Be patient

Take on adventures

Inspire/be inspired

Appreciate

Devote myself to you

Be faithful

Be true

Be kind

Remember

Uplift

Despite...

In good times and in bad

In sickness and in health

Our imperfections

Joys and sorrows

Victories and disappointments

Our changes as we grow old together

Life's challenges

For how long?

Forever.

Forever more.

All the days of my life.

For as long as I live.

For eternity.

Always.

Until heaven takes me.

For all of my days.

For as long as I breathe.

Until my last breath.

For the rest of our lives.

What is the ring? Why will you wear it?
As a symbol of continuity
As a symbol of my love, affection and faithfulness to you.
You are more precious than gold.
You'll know I'm wearing it too, wherever we are, whenever we're apart. Look at it, and know.

Checking something from each list, add a little sentence punctuation, and you've got some vows that reflect what you're feeling.

Example of a resulting vow, sample #50:

> "_____, I am so happy to share my life with you.
> You are simply, my home, my safe place...always.
>
> I promise to be that safe place for you, for the rest of our lives.
> To be patient...to cherish you...to be kind; In good times, and in bad.
>
> Wear this ring, as a symbol of my love, affection and faithfulness to you.
> And know that whenever you look at it, you'll know I'm wearing the same, and for the same reason."

In Closing

There you have it.

- Traditional Wedding Vows.
- Sample Wedding Vows.
- 10 Guides to Come Up With More

And by now, you've figured out that 50, is only the number of traditional & *original* vows in here. Include the poetry, biblical readings, Hollywood versions and others, and the book includes loads more.

So if you're still unsure of what your vows should be, it's time for more pre-marriage counseling.

While that sentence may be tongue in cheek, it's also true that you could always just say, "Live Long and Prosper". But that's not very emotional.

Here's to a Happy Marriage for you.

Good luck, many blessings, and enjoy a beautiful wedding ceremony.

Disclaimer: The author(s) have made all reasonable efforts to present "50 New & Traditional Wedding Vows plus How To Write Your Own Vows: 10 Guides " as an overview. Couples must review their vows with their legal wedding Officiant for religious or other compliance, as has been stated repeatedly throughout this book. The author(s) assume no responsibility for any particular religious order's acceptance of the reader's wedding vows, or appropriateness of the reader's sense of humor; should they attempt funny vows. Ha. Ha.

RESOURCES

[i] Gallup: Top Ten List of American's Fears
http://www.gallup.com/poll/1891/snakes-top-list-americans-fears.aspx
The Gallup Building
901 F Street, NW Washington, D.C. 20004

[ii] 1549 Book of Common Prayer
http://justus.anglican.org/resources/bcp/1549/Marriage_1549.htm
The Solemnization of Matrimony
The English Book of Common Prayer 1662
reproduced as written by John Baskerville
http://justus.anglican.org/resources/bcp/1662/baskerville.htm

[iii] Pragmaticbuddhism.org

[iv] AboutBuddhism.org
Buddhismbeliefs.org

[v] 2011 Mantstaka American Indian council
http://www.manataka.org/page25.html
Post Office Box 476
Hot Springs Reservation, AR 71902

Other Books by Marie Kay

50 Unique Wedding Readings
including Wedding Poems, Wedding Blessings & Non-religious Readings

Unique Wedding Ceremony Songs
& Where to Find Them

Made in the USA
Middletown, DE
16 September 2018